Cades Cove Wild & Free

By Dawn Wentz Bailey

First printing

Other children's books from this author include:

Joey And The Mighty Oak

Bugs On A Bus

Hog On A Log

Does Mr. Whale Have A Tail?

A special thanks goes out to my family who traveled with me on several occasions to help with the creation of this book. They took care of the driving while I was able to photograph bears, coyotes and other wildlife that forage throughout the property. I thank God for allowing me to share this wonderful experience.

Even though some of the pictures look cute and cuddly, know that these are wild animals and they are not tame. If you are out exploring nature, use binoculars or telephoto lenses to photograph and remember to keep a safe distance between you and all wildlife. Obey the rules. This is for your protection and the protection of the animals. If we take care not to overstep our boundaries with the wildlife, we will continue to have a safe and enjoyable journey at Cades Cove.

I hope families and their children enjoy the pages of this book for many years to come. May this be a testament of the beauty that abounds at Cades Cove. All wildlife included was photographed at Cades Cove, in the Great Smoky Mountains of Tennessee.

If you were a bear,

what would you do?

Would you hunt for berries:

red, black or blue?

Would you walk upon a fallen tree?

Would you walk in the water,

wild and free?

If you were a bear, would you roll
in the grass?

Would you block a deer crossing
or let him pass?

Would you get mad if a coyote

pranced by?

Would you chase it away with

an angry cry?

If you were a bear,

where would you roam?

Would you make the tree tops

part of your home?

Would you stand up straight
and hug a big tree?
Would you climb real high for
your friends to see?

If you were a bear, would you
tromp through leaves?
Would you go on a hunt
for buzzing bees?

If you were a bear,

how would you dig?

Would you use your

snout like a wild pig?

Would you slip under the fence,

beside a tree?

Would you chomp on walnuts,

wild and free?

Yes, bears eat berries:

red, black and blue.

Momma and her cubs eat

walnuts too.

Yes, bears will walk upon

fallen trees.

They drink from streams.

They are wild and free.

Yes, bears like to roll in

the tall grass.

They may warn a deer,

but let it pass.

Bears may get angry

when coyotes trot past,

though a stampede of horses

make bears run fast.

Bears like to roam in the

tops of nut trees.

They forage for walnuts to

fill their needs.

Yes, bears can stand at the base of a tree.

Their claws help them climb.

They are wild and free.

Yes, bears like to forage for

nuts amongst leaves.

They hope to find

honey from honey bees.

Yes, bears will use their
claws to climb and to dig.
They have a better sense
of smell than a pig.

Yes, bears will slip under a fence, beside a tree.

They are happy to eat walnuts.

They are wild and free.

Black Bear Facts

- Bears like to live in thick forests. They like their seclusion and like areas of mountain laurel with streams and an abundant food supply.

- Bears like to eat grass, roots, nuts, berries, honey and bugs. Sometimes they will even eat fish and other small mammals.

- You may find bears foraging through garbage cans because they have such a good sense of smell. It is said that some bears can smell food from up to 20 miles away.

- A male bear is called a boar. A female bear is called a sow. Baby bears are called cubs.

- Black bears can run about 30-35 miles per hour, so never try to outrun a bear. It is better to clap your hands and make noise.

- Usually bears are more afraid of you than you are of them, so oftentimes they will run in the other direction.

- Bears like to swim and hunt in the water.

- During the winter months, bears usually hibernate in dens made of brush piles or fallen trees. In warmer climates, you may occasionally see them out foraging for food.

Black Bear Facts

- Momma bears will usually have their babies in January when they are hibernating. The cubs only weigh about 8 ounces when they are born. Mother bears can have 1 to 6 cubs in a litter. Although, most of the time they have 2 or 3 cubs. The cubs will stay with their mother until they are about 1 1/2 years old.

- When bears are full grown, they can weigh between 150 pounds and 600 pounds. Sows usually weigh up to 200 pounds. Boars can weigh up to and sometimes exceed 600 pounds.

- A black bear's average life span is around 20 years, however, it can live up to 30 years old. This generally depends on their food supply and living conditions.

Have you learned anything new about bears?

What do you like best about black bears?

What is your favorite part of the story?

Look through the book and see which bear is your favorite.

www.ingramcontent.com/pod-product-compliance
Lightning Source LLC
Chambersburg PA
CBHW041524280526
45792CB00004B/1377